For more information address Disney Editions, 114 Fifth Avenue, New York, New York 10011-5690.

Printed in Singapore

Library of Congress Cataloging-in-Publication Data on file.

ISBN: 0-7868-5438-3

INTRODUCTION

It's 6:45 PM, and Mufasa is flying. The ushers are stuffing, the sound engineer balancing, and the box office checking their HABOS (tickets Held At Box Office), it's all in a day's work at the New Amsterdam Theatre.

For the majority of people, their first exposure to the New York City landmarked New Amsterdam Theatre occurs when they come to experience Disney's award-winning musical *The Lion King*. Yet the theatre has been home to a host of luminaries, both famous and infamous, over her century-long existence. Home of the Ziegfeld Follies, the theatre presented the likes of Will Rogers, Fanny Brice, Eddy Cantor, and Bob Hope, to name but a few. Jack Dempsey celebrated his title win in style, and the Duke of Windsor had his bachelor party on the rooftop. The theatre has weathered two world wars, the Great Depression, cinerama, and urban blight. It has witnessed countless celebrations and demonstrations in what eventually would be coined "the crossroads of the world." Still, it is as the Broadway home of *The Lion King* that the theatre is best known.

For all the spectacular effects and innovative costuming that are exposed during each performance of *The Lion King* for the public's consumption, there is another world, unknown to many, that exists just behind the velour curtains. In this hidden world, a team of unseen professionals are the reason why things work. More than a theatre, the New Am, as she is affectionately called, is a close-knit community of individuals whose contributions, be they great or small, help to create the overall theatrical experience. For every actor on stage, there are approximately four support people located behind the scenes. Some of these individuals you may see; others you may never encounter. Some begin their day when the city awakens; others arrive as the commute home begins. Most work every weekend, every holiday, every night. They work when others play.

The following photographs, shot over a 24-hour period, are the ultimate "backstage pass" to the magic of the New Am.

Nancy Amendola

Like a modern-day Harold Lloyd, engineer John Burke adjusts the massive hands of the theatre's clock perched high above 42nd Street.

TOP
The theatre seats as seen through one of the hundreds of century-old decorative grates found in the orchestra rotunda.

ABOVE
Props are stored for the night.

OPPOSITE PAGE
Mounted officer Jimmy Secreto begins his morning patrol of 42nd Street.

The New Am awakens to a new day, just the way it did over a hundred years ago. The creation of the heralded Broadway producer team of Marc Klaw and Abraham Lincoln Erlanger, the theatre was built in 1903 for an estimated $1.5 million. This was an astronomical figure for the day, considering the absolute best seat in a Broadway house went for a mere dollar.

SEQUENCE, OPPOSITE PAGE
Edmund Smith opens the 42nd Street gate. Even the terrazzo floor entranceway is landmarked.

ABOVE
One of the many underground passageways running beneath the New Amsterdam Theatre. This particular one, located in the sub cellar of the theatre, is rumored to have led to a secret exit on 41st Street during Ziegfeld's day. It provided a convenient escape route from the paparazzi gathered at the stage door.

LEFT
The New Amsterdam Theatre has a total of 6.3 miles of piping running throughout the theatre. On average, over 1,000 gallons of water and 7,500 kilowatts are utilized daily.

Reminiscent of a Rube Goldberg-esque flight of fancy, the gazelle wheel was the first concept that Julie Taymor designed to help convey "The Circle of Life" theme that runs throughout the performance.

7:00 a.m.

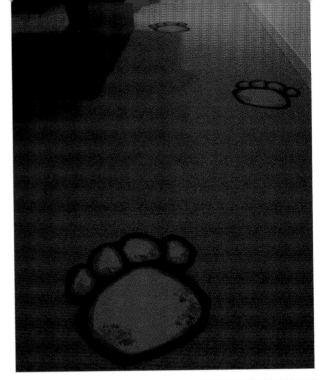

RIGHT

Images of the production abound throughout the theatre offices, even on the floor.

BELOW

One of the three water towers, located on the theatre's roof, is inspected. The towers hold a total of 20,000 gallons with two-thirds alloted to fire prevention.

TOP LEFT
The cast of *The Lion King* goes through about 200 gallons of spring water a week.

TOP RIGHT
The New Amsterdam theatre receives approximately 300 pieces of mail daily,
the most gratifying are those coming from children who have just seen the show.

ABOVE LEFT
The day maintenance crews begin to arrive.

ABOVE RIGHT
Every Monday, like clockwork, a different section of the theatre is painted.
The paint itself is carefully mixed to produce a somewhat muted version
of the original patina, making the color appear to be well preserved
instead of brand new.

Deliveries begin to arrive and will continue throughout the day. Items range from stuffed animals to dry ice, gummy grubs to programs.

8:00 a.m.

OPPOSITE PAGE

An engineer replaces a bulb in one of the curved domes of the Grand Promenade. The soft, warm glow of the ceiling is actually created by aluminum leaf that has been shellacked seven times.

BELOW

A delicate 7.5-watt bulb is replaced on one of the twenty-two art nouveau lighting sconces surrounding the orchestra section. Although part of the original 1903 decor of the theatre, none of these exquisite sconces remained when the renovation began. This, combined with a total absence of photographic records, reduced Disney designers to perusing ladies journals of the era looking for references to the "beautiful woman with a crown of lights." With just a few weeks remaining before the theatre reopened, workmen installing ductwork behind a wall literally stumbled across an old tattered box that had been shoved behind a standpipe. When opened, it revealed one of the original sconces securely wrapped in its turn-of-the-century packing. Workmen also discovered that the original lightbulbs, in their unopened boxes, worked perfectly.

8:30 a.m.

RIGHT
Armed with the bare essentials, the box office staff begins to arrive.

BELOW
Already busy, the theatre's phone room operators begin to take ticket orders; they will handle approximately 1,000 phone calls a day.

OPPOSITE PAGE
The stage door, located on 41st Street, is always a busy place. Through this portal passed the likes of Ed Wynn, Fred Astaire, and W.C. Fields, to name but a few.

20

9:00 a.m.

THIS PAGE
Standing-room locations are sold for the evening's performance to anxious guests, many of whom have been waiting patiently since early morning. (Note the aerobic step units.)

OPPOSITE PAGE
Tour guides prepare masks for the morning tour. The theatre has provided tours for a multitude of groups ranging from Brownie troops to Mikhail Gorbachev.

9:30 a.m.

RIGHT
Changing one of the 4,374 lightbulbs located throughout the theatre.

BELOW
The New Amsterdam's chief engineer Frank Gibbons crawls along the "underground railway" on his daily inspection. In actuality, it is a 100-year-old catwalk located 178 feet above the orchestra level.

OPPOSITE TOP
One of the original Ziegfeld "knockers," circa 1914. Used exclusively at the Midnight Frolic, it was found only a short distance from this catwalk.

OPPOSITE BOTTOM
A publicity shot from the Midnight Frolic. The glass runway was unique to the times.

10:00 a.m.

ABOVE
An artisan touches up one of the more than five hundred green apples that festoon the proscenium, walls, and ceilings of the theatre. The theatre, originally christened "The house beautiful," features a carved menagerie of fifty-five rabbits, forty peacocks, twenty-two squirrels, twelve monkeys, and two eagles, in addition to countless flowers and vines.

BELOW/OPPOSITE PAGE
One of the restoration team touches up the woodwork on a granite-topped bar in the main lobby. Maintaining a century-old building that hosts a steady stream of more than 750,000 guests yearly is a constant challenge. With an abundance of rehearsals, special events, and performances filling six days a week, Monday is the only "dark day" the theatre maintenance team can effect any large repairs.

10:30 a.m.

Even on the busiest days, Herlinda Feliciano still manages a ready smile.
Her next challenge is the female ensemble dressing room shown at left.

11:00 a.m.

Costumes are ironed and prepared. The wardrobe team remains active throughout the day and well into the evening dressing the actors, as well as washing, repairing, and setting out costumes.

The costume shop uses close to seventy-five different colors of thread for the production.

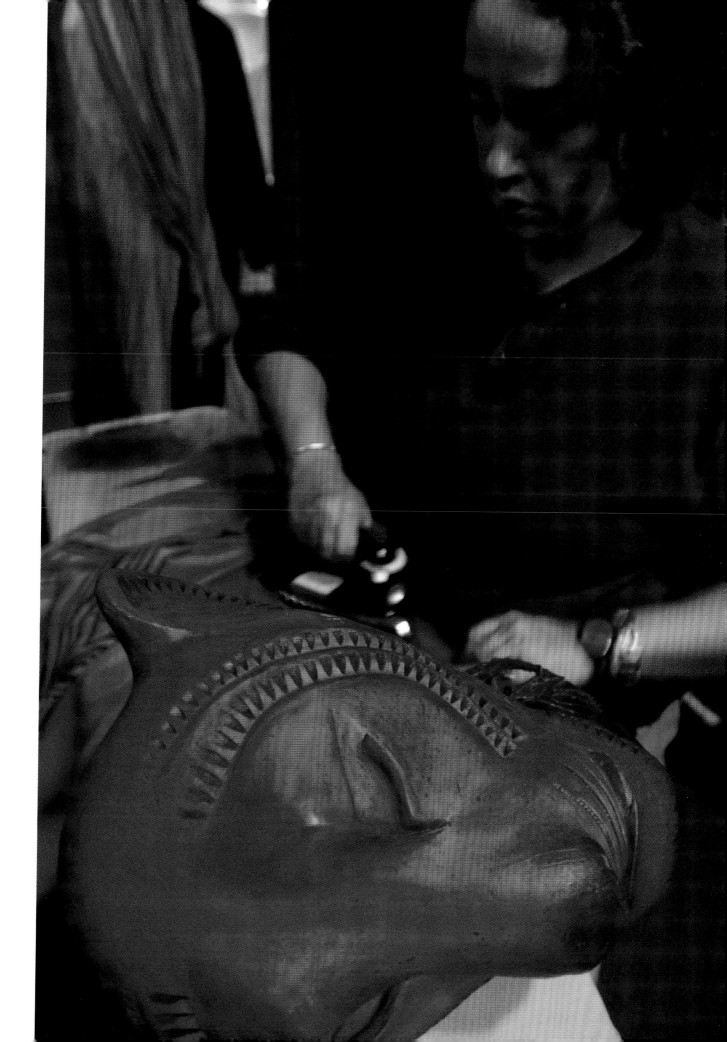

LEFT
Any article of clothing that directly touches the actor's body is sorted and washed. That translates into one hundred sixty industrial-sized loads per week. The more delicate costumes are hand cleaned daily.

BELOW LEFT
Wardrobe supervisor Kjeld Andersen inspects repairs on one of the 350 costumes he is responsible for.

BELOW RIGHT
A seamstress reattaches beads onto Rafiki's cuffs. There are countless beads utilized in the production, all hand stitched onto the bodices.

OPPOSITE PAGE
The costume crew works with a variety of materials ranging from leather to linen, silk to hemp.

DISNEY PRESENTS

THE LION KING

THE BROADWAY MUSICAL

The Script

09/01/01

Stage Adaptation

...er Allers & Irene Mecchi

...lton John

...Rice

With time constraints on everyone's mind, most employees at the New Am opt to bring lunch in, with energy bars and caffeine figuring high on the food chain.

The hair and wig department is responsible for the fifty-plus wigs and hairpieces used in the performance. In addition to traditional materials, rope, silk, and even carpets are all used in the wig construction.

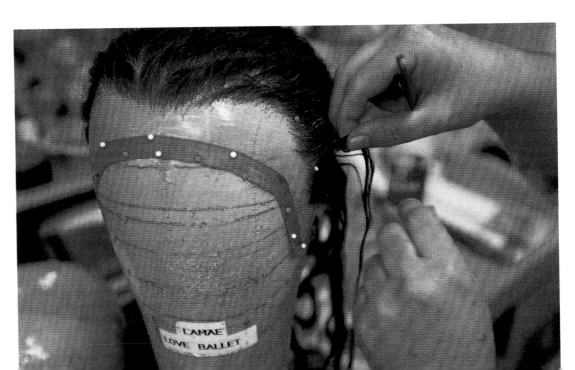

1:00 p.m.

RIGHT
The production team confers prior to the afternoon rehearsal.

BELOW
The final confrontation scene between Scar and Simba is carefully rehearsed. With the constant movement of drops, elevators, and scenery taking place simultaneously onstage, actors must be extremely confident in their blocking.

Complaint Department

* Press button for service.

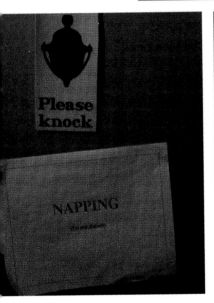

Please knock

NAPPING

314

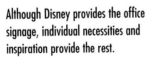

Although Disney provides the office signage, individual necessities and inspiration provide the rest.

HIPPIES
→USE→
SIDE DOOR

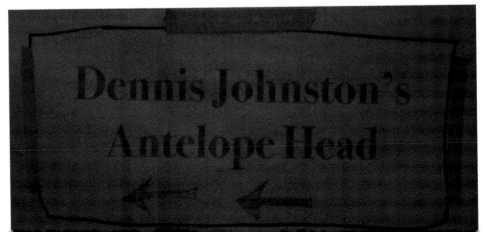

Dennis Johnston's Antelope Head

STRUCTURE OF THE ROAD CREW

THE CARPENTER:
LEAPS OVER TALL BUILDINGS IN A SINGLE BOUND.
IS MORE POWERFUL THAN A LOCOMOTIVE.
IS FASTER THAN A SPEEDING BULLET.
WALKS ON WATER.
GIVES POLICY TO GOD.

THE ELECTRICIAN:
LEAPS OVER SHORT BUILDINGS IN A SINGLE BOUND.
IS MORE POWERFUL THAN A SWITCH ENGINE.
IS ALMOST AS FAST AS A SPEEDING BULLET.
WALKS ON WATER IF THE SEA IS CALM AND THE ELECTRIC SERVICE IS OFF.
OCCASIONALLY TALKS WITH GOD IF HE THINKS NO ONE IS LISTENING.

THE PROPERTY MAN:
LEAPS OVER SHORT BUILDINGS WITH A RUNNING START AND FAVORABLE TAIL WIND.
IS NOT AS POWERFUL AS A SWITCH ENGINE.
IS FASTER THAN A SPEEDING BB.
WALKS ON WATER IN THE SHALLOW END OF AN INDOOR SWIMMING POOL.
TALKS TO GOD IF A SPECIAL REQUEST IS APPROVED BY THE GENERAL OFFICE.

THE ASSISTANT ELECTRICIAN:
BARELY CLEARS A QUONSET HUT.
LOSES TUG OF WAR WITH SWITCH ENGINE.
CAN FIRE A SPEEDING BULLET.
SWIMS WELL IN WATER.
IS OCCASIONALLY ADDRESSED BY GOD BUT NEVER WHILE ELECTRICIAN IS PRESENT.

THE SOUND MAN:
MAKES SCUFF MARKS ON THE WALL WHEN TRYING TO LEAP OVER BUILDINGS.
CAN SOMETIMES HANDLE FIREARM WITHOUT INFLICTING SELF-INJURY.
DOGPADDLES WELL IN WATER.
TALKS IN MANNER WHICH SOUNDS REMARKABLY LIKE A FEED-BACK.

THE FRONT LAMP MAN:
RUNS INTO BUILDINGS.
RECOGNIZES SWITCH ENGINE TWO OUT OF THREE TIMES IF AIDED BY HEADSET.
IS NEVER ISSUED EITHER LIVE OR BLANK AMMUNITION.
CAN SOMETIMES STAY AFLOAT WITH A LIFE PRESERVER.
TALKS TO WALLS.

THE FLYMAN:
FALLS OVER DOORSTEPS WHEN TRYING TO ENTER BUILDINGS.
SAYS, "LOOK AT THE CHOO-CHOO."
PLAYS IN MUD PUDDLES.
WETS HIMSELF WITH A WATER PISTOL.
TALKS TO HIMSELF.

THE WARDROBE MISTRESS:
LIFTS BUILDINGS AND WALKS UNDER THEM.
KICKS LOCOMOTIVES OFF THE TRACK.
CATCHES SPEEDING BULLETS IN HER TEETH AND EATS THEM.
FREEZES WATER WITH A SINGLE GLANCE.
SHE IS GOD.

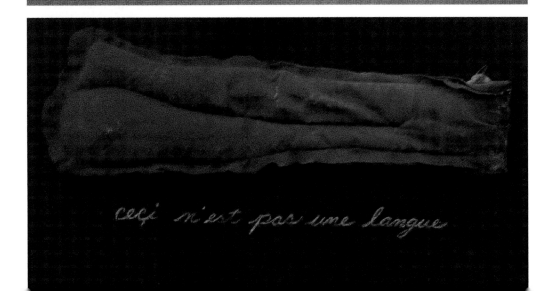

ceci n'est pas une langue

TOP
After signing in for rehearsal Keswa and Lamae strike a pose.

ABOVE
Stage manger Jimmie Lee calls actors to stage.

RIGHT
Timon proves you can run, but you cannot hide.

OPPOSITE PAGE
Resident director Brian Hill prepares Leon Thomas, age eleven, for his first Broadway performance.

With rehearsal in full swing, dancers practice their choreography for the lioness hunt scene. In addition to the regularly scheduled eight-performance week, there are also rehearsals, voice work, and costume fittings scheduled each day.

OPPOSITE PAGE
Sheila Little-Terrell adjusts Tony James's bodice.

LEFT
One of the wardrobe crew carries a load of hyena legs to the stage. The company uses more than a hundred pairs of shoes ranging from dance shoes to combat boots.

BELOW
Head electrician Jimmie Maloney prepares to ascend to the lighting grid. If every light associated with the production was switched on simultaneously they would draw in excess of a million watts.

FAR BELOW
Paul Ascenzo accompanies the rehearsal on keyboard. There are a total of twenty-three musicians, plus a conductor, involved with the production. In addition to traditional instruments, percussionists for *The Lion King* play a host of exotic items including: djembe, talking drum, mbira, djun-djun, berimbau, k'panlogo and gyil.

THIS PAGE

The puppetry department takes on the flavor of Frankenstein's laboratory as heads, hands, and torsos are disassembled and reattached at will. Most every puppet that appears on stage has a backup behind the scenes.

OPPOSITE PAGE

Timon gets a quick dental checkup prior to showtime.

4:00 p.m.

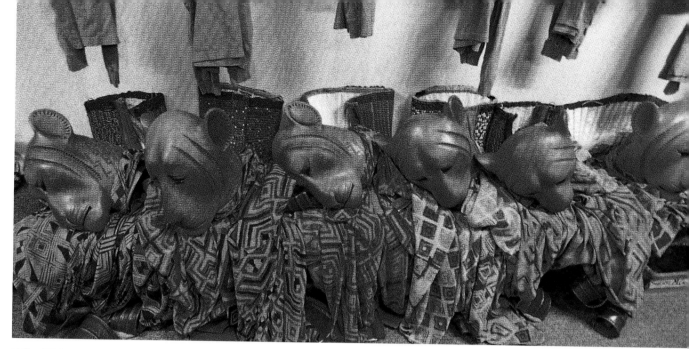

ABOVE
All headpieces are constructed from carbon graphite. In its liquid form it can be poured into molds and when dry yields an extremely lightweight yet durable finished product. This is the same material that is used in stealth aircraft and space shuttle components.

LEFT
A stagehand checks the well-used fly system during rehearsal. With scenery, electrics, special effects, and even costumes suspended, virtually every inch of the fly space is utilized.

OPPOSITE PAGE
Giraffe heads find a spot to live in the center of a staircase. With real estate at a premium backstage, every open nook and cranny of the theatre becomes valuable property.

ABOVE
Unique to the New Amsterdam Theatre, ushers' name tags reflect the owner's pride in their individual neighborhoods.

BELOW
Usher's costumes returned from dry cleaning. To promote the concept of being on stage, and thus promoting a higher degree of guest service, employees are referred to as cast members and uniforms are referred to as costumes.

OPPOSITE PAGE
One of the century-old porcelain glazed terra-cotta banisters gets the once-over before the audience arrives. The newel posts feature carved reliefs of Shakespearean characters, while the balustrades contain a virtual menagerie of animals taken from the children's fables of Aesop and Hans Christian Andersen.

5:00 p.m.

THIS PAGE
During a dinner break, the surviving members of the Ziegfeld Follies arrive for a dedication ceremony celebrating the theatre's centennial. Billy Blanchard (age 98), right, posing with her original publicity photo, and Doris Eaton Travis (age 99) help cut the ribbon, while Florenz Ziegfeld, their former boss, looks on approvingly from his place on the wall.

OPPOSITE
Doris Eaton and her baby brother Charlie visit what is left of the rooftop theatre located above the main stage. The theatre began life as a supper club in the early 1900s and grew into New York's premier nightspot through the late twenties.

OPPOSITE PAGE
Merchandise stands become active as cast members prepare for the evening's performance.

TOP
Assistant company manager, Laura Eichholz, is a welcome sight tonight as she hands Ruthlyn Solomons, the resident dance instructor, her paycheck.

MIDDLE
During dinner break, stagehands share a few ribald stories.

BOTTOM
Soundman Scott Stauffer conducts a preshow sound check. The sound department has thirty minutes to check eighty-seven different microphones and ninety-seven different speakers.

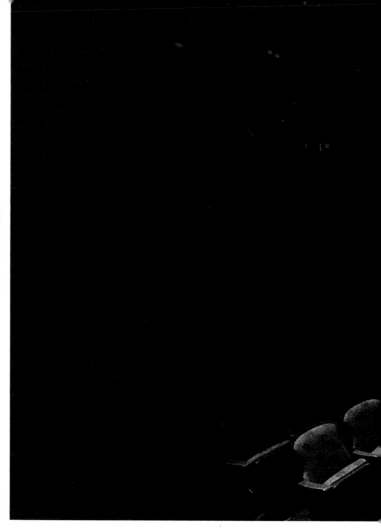

LEFT
A liquid nitrogen geyser is tested preshow.

TOP CENTER
Bird ladies headpieces are preset at the front of house.

FAR RIGHT
A stagehand hurries across the stage during lighting check.

RIGHT TOP
Ushers begin photocopying any cast changes behind one
of the theatre's art nouveau doors.

RIGHT
Concession-stand staff begin their load-in as cups are
carefully counted.

6:30 p.m.

Lots of small alcoves in the theatre come alive with ushers stuffing cast changes into programs. Very much a social event, it affords the perfect opportunity to catch up on the latest theatre gossip.

BELOW

Bertha, the production's largest animal, makes her nightly trek from her backstage compound to the front of house with the help of property head Victor Amerling accompanied by five burly stagehands. Although massive in appearance, she only weighs in at fifty pounds. (The camera always adds a few pounds.)

7:00 p.m.

THIS PAGE

It's 7:20 P.M.; do you know where your tickets are? With hundreds of HABOs (literally tickets that are "Held At Box Office" to be picked up the night of show), Harry Jaffie, one of the New Am treasurers, copes with the unending rush of anxious guests, all who seem to arrive at the last possible second.

OPPOSITE TOP

Costumes laid out neatly in the sub-stage quick change room, referred to as "the Bunker," take on an almost spiritual quality in one of the only areas in the theatre that remains tranquil preshow.

OPPOSITE BOTTOM

With a lion's share of work yet to accomplish, one of the wardrobe team takes a quick breather.

7:15 p.m.

THIS PAGE

Production makeup supervisor Elizabeth Cohen (upper right) and her two person staff have a daunting job ahead of them. In less than an hour they must apply the complicated facial designs to virtually all of the major characters. Scar's makeup alone takes close to forty-five minutes. Once, the understudy for Rafiki had to go on unexpectedly mid-show, meaning that a character that usually takes thirty minutes to complete was made-up, mic'd and dressed in a total of six, just in time for her next entrance!

OPPOSITE PAGE

Adam Stein (Zazu) is one of the first actors to be made up, his next stop is wardrobe.

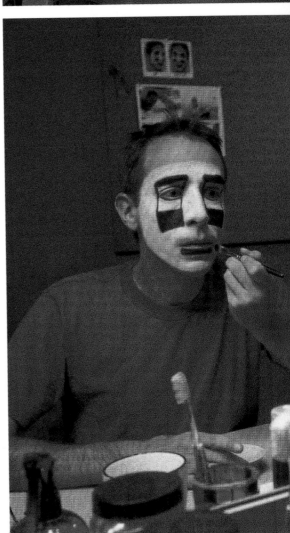

7:30 p.m.

Sporting their white robes, dancers arrive on the stage and begin to warm up as dressers, stagehands, and stage managers make last-minute preparations.

TOP

On the other side of the show curtain, the presence of an audience can now be felt by cast and crew alike.

ABOVE AND LEFT

As ushers seat the last few guests, the actors get into their costumes in preparation for the opening procession.

Most guests have no idea of the frenzy of hidden activity that is occurring around them.

69

8:00 p.m.

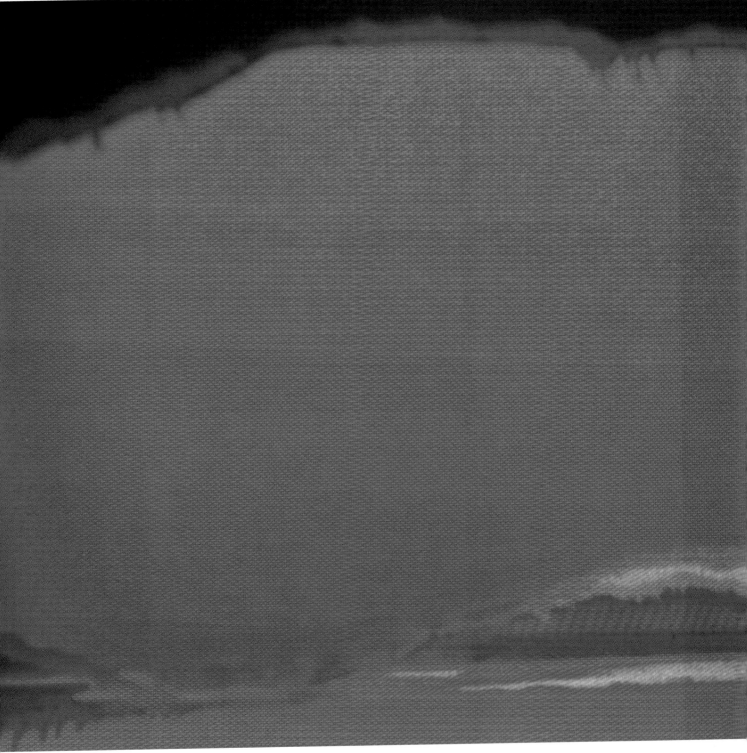

RIGHT
Nomvula Dlamini in the role of Rafiki takes a quiet moment and collects her thoughts prior to her opening chant. Unlike traditional Broadway musicals, *The Lion King* begins cold, that is sans overture. Nomvula must hit her first note dead on every night, or the entire opening act will be off.

BELOW
A last minute on-stage stretch before the curtain rises.

BELOW
Performers make their way through the audience toward the stage.

OPPOSITE PAGE
A zebra walks onto the warm glow of the stage during "The Circle of Life."

TOP
A giraffe stoically waits stage right for his entrance.

ABOVE
A flyman raises the curtain, pretty much the same way it was done in 1903.

With only inches to spare, actors, dressers, stagehands, stage managers, props and sets pieces all move rhythmically in an intricate ballet, just out of sight of the audience.

TOP

Mufasa gets Simba's adrenaline going before his entrance.

OPPOSITE PAGE

Ten-year-old Danny Fetter prepares for his Broadway debut. He is accompanied by Nicole White, the child wrangler for the show. To date, more than thirty children have made their Broadway debut with the New York company of *The Lion King*.

8:40 p.m.

TOP
While the show goes on, the business of the theatre takes place in the box office where the treasurer, company manager, and house manager review the nightly ticket statement.

ABOVE
Bertha, the elephant, is quietly raised into the rafters stage right, just a few feet from the action on stage.

OPPOSITE PAGE
The bunker, which forty minutes ago was as peaceful as a church, comes alive with quick changes.

8:50 p.m.

THIS PAGE

Steve Stackle controls the automation system for Pride Rock. Located directly below the stage, monitors allow him to observe what is occurring just a few feet above him.

OPPOSITE PAGE

Actors manipulate shadow puppets prior to their stage entrance.

Intermission

ABOVE LEFT
The stage manager's office takes on the air of an air-traffic control tower during the fifteen-minute intermission.

ABOVE RIGHT/RIGHT
Ticket takers prepare for the deluge of audience members as actors rush to their dressing rooms.

OPPOSITE PAGE
Stagehands busily reset Rafiki's tree, deflate rubber cacti, and spread out water silk.

9:35 p.m.

It's the top of Act 2, and the theatre becomes an aviary as bird kites take to the sky, controlled by actors scattered about the audience.

9:45 p.m.

Actors perform "One by One" on a stage that has been automatically raked.

ABOVE
A stagehand attaches the Timon puppet to his branch in preparation of the waterfall scene. There are over 250 puppets in *The Lion King*, a virtual alphabet soup from ants to zebras.

OPPOSITE
Derek Smith, as Scar, watches one of the numerous monitors located offstage while waiting for his entrance. His costume is the most complicated in the show. It is constructed almost entirely of leather and is fitted with several small motors that he uses to control his headpiece.

10:00 p.m.

ABOVE
One of the hyenas steals a quiet moment to rest between scenes.

BELOW
Simba prepares for his entrance.

OPPOSITE PAGE
Original company members Jason Raize (Simba) and Heather Headley (Nala) perform "Can You Feel the Love Tonight?" as sinuous dancers, both onstage and dangling high above, blossom into a lush jungle.

OPPOSITE PAGE

Trust personified: stagehands literally have the lives of the onstage flyers in their hands.

SEQUENCE THIS PAGE

John Brady, portraying Timon, has approximately twenty seconds to exit the waterfall scene, take an elevator to his position under the stage, and reappear via the downstage elevator.

Even a few seconds' delay will feel like an eternity to the actors still on stage awaiting his line.

LEFT/ABOVE
During act 2, young Simba and Nala have plenty of time to complete their nightly homework assignments before their curtain call, although "occasionally" they are distracted. The children, ranging in age from eight to twelve, are a constant source of joy for all involved with the production. There are a total of four children, two boys and two girls, who alternate the roles of Simba and Nala.

BELOW
One of the hyenas takes a well-deserved break in his dressing room. The demands put on the actors' bodies during the performance makes the company's physical therapist a popular person.

OPPOSITE
The continually updated growth chart is scribbled on the wall by a steady progression of young lions.

KAREN 5/17/98

Sonya 11-17-00

Cay 5/17/98

Scott 5/17/99

Jeremy 9/14/01

ast day (88)

Ian 1-7-00

Kristen 2/9/00

Jen 5/17/98   KEITH 2-13-03

Julissa   Kristen 2.9.00   Ian 2.9.00
2.9.00

IVAN

Derek 8-10-02

Natasha
7.7.97

Kiah 2 5:05 Ashley 5/20/98   IVAN

Jeremy 8/16/00

10:30 p.m.

Tom Robbins, who originated the role of Pumbaa, gets a last-minute touch-up illuminated by a "bite light," in layman's terms: an ordinary plastic key-chain light. With seconds between entrances, dressers don't have the luxury to escort actors to well-lit dressing rooms, so they adjust costumes and touch up makeup on the fly with these little lights clenched firmly between their teeth.

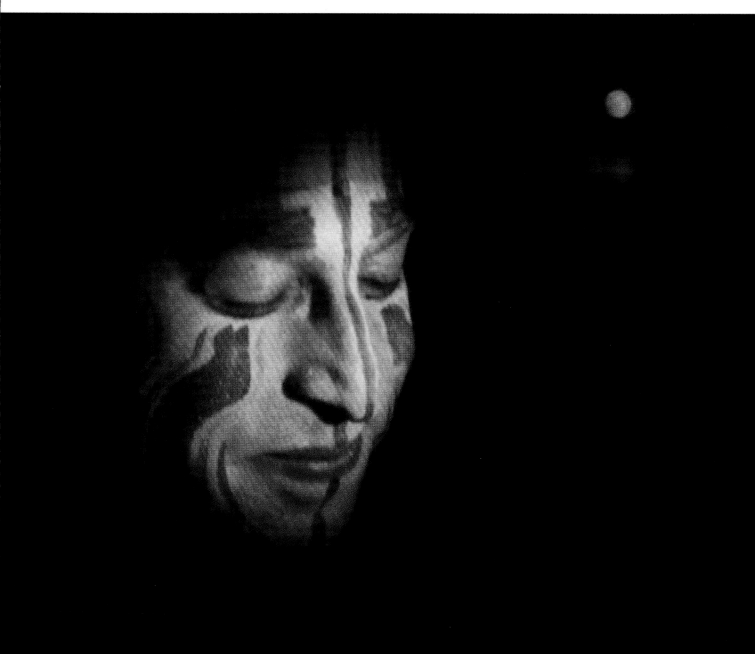

ABOVE
Pumbaa awaits his cue.

ABOVE RIGHT
An actor makes a quick run from the front of house to the rear of house, passing behind audience members without being noticed.

OPPOSITE RIGHT
Simba as seen from the wings.

OVERLEAF
With stagehands supporting the sky walk set piece, Simba and Scar, supported by flying harnesses, stage their long awaited final confrontation.

LEFT/SEQUENCE BELOW
With the help of a stepladder, the giraffes become human again.

OPPOSITE TOP/UPPER RIGHT
"And they're off ..." With the final curtain call over, the race is on to get out of costumes and makeup. Preparations that may have taken an hour preshow are completely removed in a matter of minutes.

BELOW
Zazu, who seems to be a bit perturbed at the sudden intrusion, gets a quick postperformance checkup by Bo Metzler.

OPPOSITE TOP
Security host Juan Hernandez monitors 41st Street as the actors depart the building.

OPPOSITE BOTTOM
With another performance complete, the backstage areas come alive with laughter.

BELOW
Wildebeest rollers are brought out on stage and inspected. The delicate mechanisms of the stage machinery must be constantly inspected to ensure a smooth performance during showtime.

Stagehands work into the night as the automation of Pride Rock is tested.

ABOVE
Head carpenter Drew Siccardi executes a quick touch up.

12:30 a.m.

As if trying to sandbag the course of a mighty river Claudia McLeod cleans and stacks booster cushions in preparation for tomorrow's matinee.

BELOW

Mufasa and Simba's dressing room takes on the air of a sacred temple in the early morning hours.

Photographs of lions, stuffed animals, fan letters, and a shadowy photograph of a long-departed Ziegfeld girl all have special significance.

RIGHT

Two Ziegfeld girls from the turn-of-century flee the confines of their dressing room and opt to apply makeup "al fresco" on the fire escape.

BELOW LEFT
"Lady Progress" receives a thorough dusting. Before the Disney restoration team brought the New Am back to its original splendor, almost all of the wall reliefs were spray painted chocolate brown. This was done to decrease reflective light when the theatre was converted into a movie house, starting with B-grade films in the 1930s and ending with Kung Fu flicks in the 1980s.

BELOW RIGHT
The detailed ceiling of the theatre takes on the appearance of a hovering starship in the early-morning hours. If you look closely, you can see four muses on swings depicting the points of the compass.

Armed with his portable vacuum backpack, Miguel Rodriguez makes his way through all 1,801 seats of the theatre. Over the years exiting guests have left behind myriad treasures, discovered by late-night cleaning crews, ranging from diamond rings to dentures!

2:40 a.m.

Batteries are replaced on the wall clocks weekly. With traveling companies on tour around the globe, the moon never sets on *The Lion King*.

A lone security guard goes on his nightly rounds. The unoccupied rooftop theatre is a bit daunting this time of night, especially with rumors, along with occasional sightings, of former Ziegfeld girl Olive Thomas.

4:00 a.m.

RIGHT

A twenty-gallon freshwater aquarium located under stage left provides a touch of home and tranquility. Maintained by the Pride Rock technician, eight to ten tetras call this home.

BELOW

Celebrities, dignitaries, and notable personalities sign one of the backstage walls in what has become a tradition at the New Amsterdam Theatre. Names run the gamut from Arnold Schwarzenegger to Maya Angelou.

5:00 a.m.

With only one job left before he heads for home, a night porter cleans the sidewalk on 41st Street as dawn slowly breaks over Manhattan—and the entire process begins again.

PHOTO CREDITS

All photographs by Gino Domenico except:

Page 110: Diane Marino

Pages 25, 111, and 120: White Studios

ACKNOWLEDGMENTS

The author and photographer would like to thank the following people—without them this book would not have been possible:

Thomas Schumacher

Wendy Lefkon

Alex Eiserloh

Nils Hansen

The Ziegfeld Club

Alan Levey

Dave Ehle

Kjeld Andersen

Louis Troisi

Landmark Signs

Guardian

Penguin

Securitas

El Digito

The New York City Police Department

The entire New York cast and crew of *The Lion King*,
    and the unions that represent them

The entire staff of The New Amsterdam Theatre